EYE OPENERS

Clothing

BLACKBIRCH®
PRESS

San Diego • Detroit • New York • San Francisco • Cleveland
New Haven, Conn. • Waterville, Maine • London • Munich

Photo credits: pages 4, 6, 10, 22 © CORBIS; pages 8, 12, 14, 18, 20 © Corel Corporation; page 16 © Digital Stock

LIBRARY OF CONGRESS CATALOGING-IN-PUBLICATION DATA

Nathan, Emma.
  Clothing / by Emma Nathan.
    p. cm. — (Eyeopeners series)
Summary: Introduces clothing worn in different parts of the world, including simple robes worn by Tibetan monks and colorful kente cloth worn by men and women in Ghana.
Includes bibliographical references.
  ISBN 1-56711-597-7 (hardback : alk. paper)
  1. Costume—Juvenile literature. 2. Clothing and dress—Juvenile literature. [1. Clothing and dress.] I. Title.

GT518 .N38 2003
391—dc21   2002012468

Printed in United States
10 9 8 7 6 5 4 3 2 1

TABLE OF CONTENTS

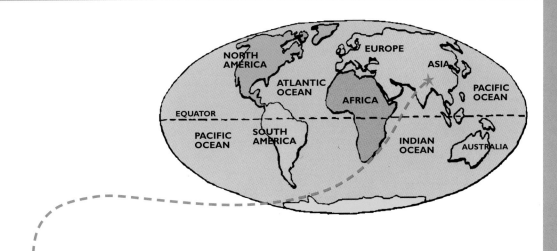

NEPAL (nuh-PAHL)

Nepal is on the continent of Asia.

It is a small country between India and China.

There are many high mountains in Nepal. The air is cool high in the mountains.

People in the mountains wear wool clothes to keep them warm.

◀ **Nepali girl**

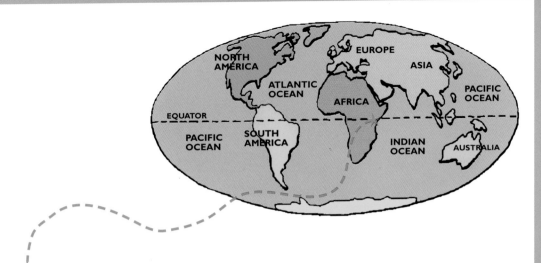

KENYA (KEN-yuh)

Kenya is on the continent of Africa.

The country is near the middle of Africa.

Kenya lies on the equator. The hottest places in the world lie on the equator.

The Masai (muh-SY) are native peoples of Kenya.

They wear loose clothes to stay cool.

◀ **Two Masai men from Kenya**

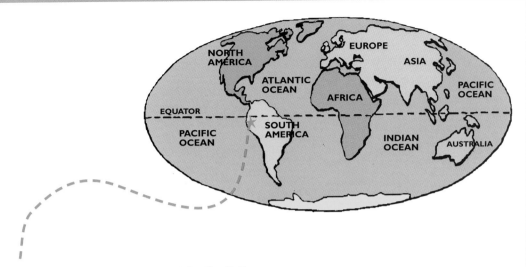

PERU (peh-ROO)

Peru is on the continent of South America.

The high mountains of the Andes (AN-deez) run from the top of Peru to the bottom.

Many mountain people in Peru herd llamas.

They use wool from the llamas to make their clothes.

Many women wear hats. The style of a hat tells others where she is from.

◀ **Woman and child in Peru with a llama**

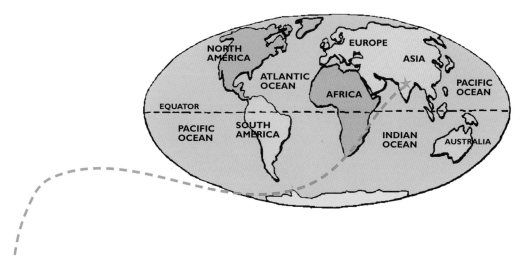

INDIA (IN-dee-ya)

India is on the continent of Asia.

Much of India is very hot.

Many women in India wear a colorful loose cloth called a sari (SAR-ee).

Many men wear a cloth on their heads, called a turban.

◀ **Indian man with a yellow turban**

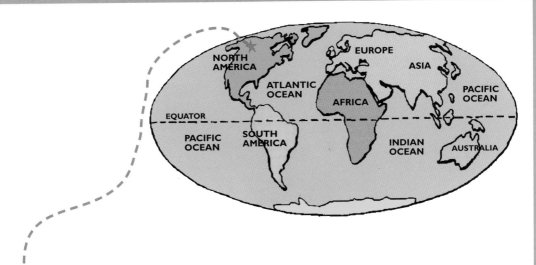

CANADA (CAN-a-duh)

Canada is on the continent of North America.

Much of the country is wilderness. Many plants and animals live in Canada's wilderness.

Canada has been home to Native Americans for thousands of years.

Traditional Native Americans used feathers and furs from Canada's many animals to make clothing.

◀ Native American in Canada

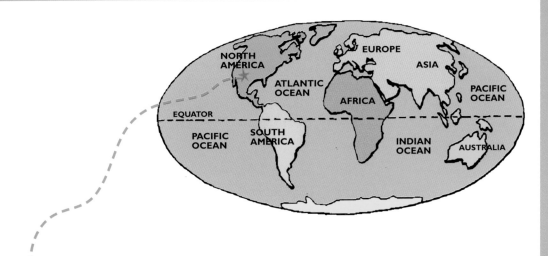

UNITED STATES (yu-nye-ted STAYTS)

The United States is on the continent of North America.

Much of the United States is flat lands, called plains.

Cowboys on horseback have traditionally herded cattle across the plains.

Cowboys ride horses while they herd cattle.

Cowboys wear leather flaps on their pants called chaps. Chaps protect their pants while the cowboys ride.

◀ Cowboy

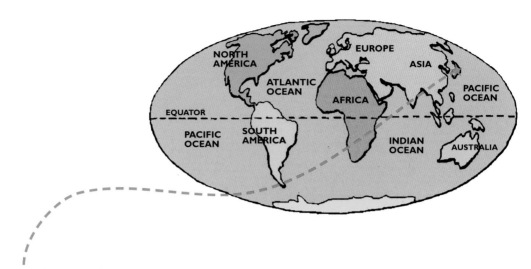

JAPAN (jah-PAN)

Japan is an island that is part of Asia.

Many people in Japan still follow customs that are thousands of years old.

In Japan a traditional servant woman is called a geisha (GAY-shuh).

A geisha wears a silk robe called a kimono (kih-MO-no).

Geishas also paint their faces white and paint their lips red.

◀ Geisha

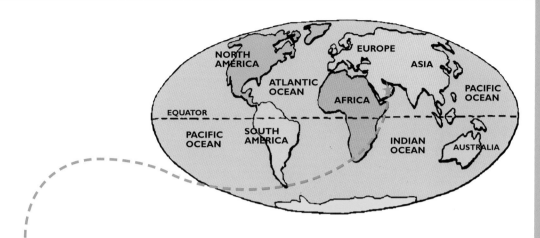

SAUDI ARABIA
(SOW-dee a-RAY-bee-ya)

Saudi Arabia is on the continent of Asia.
It is in an area called the Middle East.

Much of Saudi Arabia is desert.

Traditional Saudi clothing is loose fitting
so people stay cool.

Many Saudi men wear a piece of cloth on
their heads called a *kaffiyeh* (kuh-FEE-yuh).

Kaffiyehs help to protect against sun
and wind.

◀ **Saudi man wearing a *kaffiyeh***

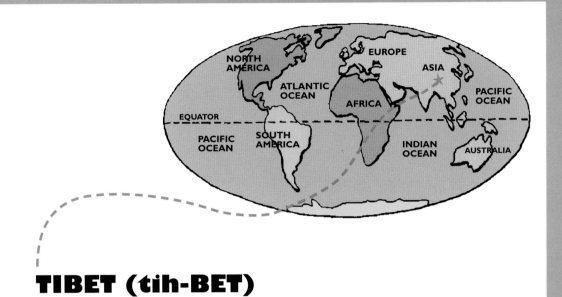

TIBET (tih-BET)

Tibet is on the continent of Asia.

It is a small country that has long been ruled by China.

Most people in Tibet belong to a religion called Buddhism (BOO-diz-um).

Buddhists believe that clothing should be very simple.

Buddhist monks and nuns in Tibet wear simple bright red or yellow robes.

◀ **Monks in Tibet**

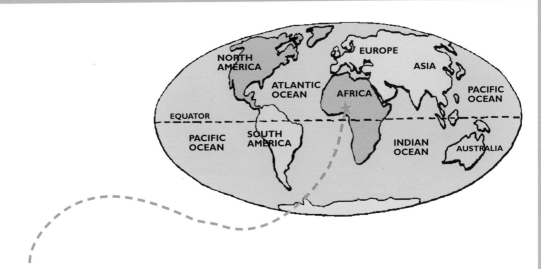

GHANA (GAH-nuh)

Ghana is on the continent of Africa.

Ghana is near the equator. It is very hot in Ghana.

The traditional clothes of Ghana are loose-fitting to help people stay cool.

Women wear colorful wraparound skirts and head scarves.

Many men wear traditional cloth robes called *kente* (ken-TAY).

◀ **Woman wearing a traditional head wrap**

Index

For More Information

Websites

Ethnic Costumes
http://www.costumes.org/pages/ethnolnk.htm

Traditional Clothing from Around the World
http://www.rice.edu/projects/topics/internatl/
traditional-clothing.htm

Books

Hall, Margaret C. *Clothing Around the World.* Chicago: Heinemann, 2001.

MacDonald, Fiona. *Clothing and Jewelry: Discovering World Cultures.* New York: Crabtree Publishing, 2001.